Join Our Team
Achieve a Dream
Knowledge Changes You
You Change the World

SMART@GRADES
NEXT EVOLUTION BRAIN POWER REVOLUTION

What's Inside?

✓ Academic Calendar

✓ Take Great Textbook Notes

✓ Active Listening Skills

✓ Write Daily Test Review Notes

✓ Use Association Cues for Instant and Total Recall

✓ Convert Facts into Test Questions

✓ Review for Retention, Recognition, and Recall

✓ Self-Test for Instant and Total Recall

✓ Power Study Snacks

WE ARE THE FUTURE
EVERYBODY IS SOMEBODY SPECIAL

SMARTGRADES Due Dates

Academic Calendar: August-January

August

| Class | What's Due? | Due Date |

Back to School: Get Organized, Prepare Study Room, Purchase School Supplies

----

September

_____

October

November

December

January

SMARTGRADES Due Dates

SMARTGRADES: NEXT EVOLUTION BRAIN POWER REVOLUTION

Academic Calendar: February-June

February Class	**What's Due?**	**Due Date**
------------------------	------------------------	------------------------
------------------------	------------------------	------------------------
------------------------	------------------------	------------------------

March

------------------------	------------------------	------------------------
------------------------	------------------------	------------------------
------------------------	------------------------	------------------------

April

------------------------	------------------------	------------------------
------------------------	------------------------	------------------------
------------------------	------------------------	------------------------

May

------------------------	------------------------	------------------------
------------------------	------------------------	------------------------
------------------------	------------------------	------------------------

June

------------------------	------------------------	------------------------
------------------------	------------------------	------------------------
------------------------	------------------------	------------------------

@2000. All Rights Reserved. **SMARTGRADES INC.**

SMARTGRADES:WE ARE THE FUTURE

Take Control of Your Day, Your Dream, and Your Destiny!

SMARTGRADES:NEXT EVOLUTION BRAIN POWER REVOLUTION

How to Read a Textbook, Write Test Review Notes and Ace the Exam

1. Choose a study area that is free of external and social distractions: _____ ✔

2. Eat a **Power Study Snack** to stay energized and focused (see list): _____ ✔

3. **Manage your time.** ✔
   Estimate Time (Fantasy):   Start Time: Finish Time: **Actual Time (Reality):**

4. **Divide and Conquer:** Read one paragraph at a time. ✔
   Active Reading: Read a paragraph and underline the <u>main idea</u> and <u>supporting details.</u> ✔

5. Condensation (Distillation): Outline/summarize your textbook into **Test Review Notes.** ✔

6. Do the facts need further clarification (see another textbook, tutoring center, or teacher)? ✔

7. **Visualize the test question.** Convert the facts into a test question: Define the Term? Compare? Contrast? Cause and Effect? Pros and Cons? List? Prove? Discuss? Outline? Agree or Disagree? ✔

8. Use **Association Cues** to memorize facts for **Instant and Total Recall.** Attach an unknown fact to a known fact stored in your memory. Use very personal memories for higher rates of retention. ✔

Acrostic Cue: Use a sentence to condense the key facts. For example, to remember the order of G-clef notes on sheet music, (E, G, B, D, F,) use the classic acrostic: Every Good Boy Deserves Fun.

Rhyme Cue: Use rhymes to link the key facts together. For example, the classic,"I before E, except after C."

Music Cue: Make up a song or poem with the information in it. Sing the song or recite the poem several times.

Chaining Cue: Create a story where each word or idea you have to remember cues the next idea you need to recall. Use your imagination. If you had to remember the name, Shirley Temple, you could rhyme Shirley with curly and remember that she had curly hair around her temples.

Funny Cue: Write a joke that contains the key facts. The funniest, most outlandish, and the strangest concoction of memory cues makes memorizing easy.

9. Two weeks before the test, **Self-Test** for strengths and weaknesses (change weak cues). ✔

10. The day of the test, review your study notes to refresh your memory. **Ace the Test.** ✔

SMARTGRADES: WE ARE THE FUTURE

Date:
Chapter:
Divide and Conquer: Read One Paragraph at a Time. Number the Paragraphs.
Paragraph #
Step 1. What is the Main Idea:

_____
_____

Step 2. List Supporting Details/Examples/Arguments:

_____
_____
_____
_____
_____
_____

Step 3. Visualize the Test Question. Convert the Facts into a Test Question: Who? What? When? Where? Why?

_____
_____

Paragraph #
Step 1. What is the Main Idea:

_____
_____

Step 2. List Supporting Details/Examples/Arguments:

_____
_____
_____
_____
_____
_____

Step 3. Visualize the Test Question. Convert the Facts into a Test Question: Who? What? When? Why? Where?

_____
_____

SMARTGRADES: NEXT EVOLUTION BRAIN POWER REVOLUTION

Step 4. To Ace the Test, Use Association Cues to Memorize Facts for Instant and Total Recall.

Step 5: Self-Test for Strengths and Weaknesses (Change Weak Association Cues).

					List Fact and Memory Association Cue

SMARTGRADES: WE ARE THE FUTURE

Date:
Chapter:
Divide and Conquer: Read One Paragraph at a Time. Number the Paragraphs.
Paragraph #
Step 1. What is the Main Idea:

_____
_____

Step 2. List Supporting Details/Examples/Arguments:

_____
_____
_____
_____
_____
_____

Step 3. Visualize the Test Question. Convert the Facts into a Test Question: Who? What? When? Where? Why?

_____
_____

Paragraph #
Step 1. What is the Main Idea:

_____
_____

Step 2. List Supporting Details/Examples/Arguments:

_____
_____
_____
_____
_____
_____

Step 3. Visualize the Test Question. Convert the Facts into a Test Question: Who? What? When? Why? Where?

_____
_____

SMARTGRADES: NEXT EVOLUTION BRAIN POWER REVOLUTION

Step 4. To Ace the Test, Use Association Cues to Memorize Facts for Instant and Total Recall.

Step 5: Self-Test for Strengths and Weaknesses (Change Weak Association Cues).

List Fact and Memory Association Cue

SMARTGRADES: WE ARE THE FUTURE

Date:
Chapter:
Divide and Conquer: Read One Paragraph at a Time. Number the Paragraphs.
Paragraph #
Step 1. What is the Main Idea:

___

Step 2. List Supporting Details/Examples/Arguments:

___

Step 3. Visualize the Test Question. Convert the Facts into a Test Question: Who? What? When? Where? Why?

___

Paragraph #
Step 1. What is the Main Idea:

___

Step 2. List Supporting Details/Examples/Arguments:

___

Step 3. Visualize the Test Question. Convert the Facts into a Test Question: Who? What? When? Why? Where?

___

SMARTGRADES: NEXT EVOLUTION BRAIN POWER REVOLUTION

Step 4. To Ace the Test, Use Association Cues to Memorize Facts for Instant and Total Recall.

Step 5: Self-Test for Strengths and Weaknesses (Change Weak Association Cues).

List Fact and Memory Association Cue

SMARTGRADES: WE ARE THE FUTURE

Date:
Chapter:
Divide and Conquer: Read One Paragraph at a Time. Number the Paragraphs.
Paragraph #
Step 1. What is the Main Idea:

_____
_____

Step 2. List Supporting Details/Examples/Arguments:

_____
_____
_____
_____
_____
_____

Step 3. Visualize the Test Question. Convert the Facts into a Test Question: Who? What? When? Where? Why?

_____
_____

Paragraph #
Step 1. What is the Main Idea:

_____
_____

Step 2. List Supporting Details/Examples/Arguments:

_____
_____
_____
_____
_____
_____

Step 3. Visualize the Test Question. Convert the Facts into a Test Question: Who? What? When? Why? Where?

_____
_____

SMARTGRADES: NEXT EVOLUTION BRAIN POWER REVOLUTION

Step 4. To Ace the Test, Use Association Cues to Memorize Facts for Instant and Total Recall.

Step 5: Self-Test for Strengths and Weaknesses (Change Weak Association Cues).

List Fact and Memory Association Cue

SMARTGRADES: WE ARE THE FUTURE

Date:
Chapter:
Divide and Conquer: Read One Paragraph at a Time. Number the Paragraphs.
Paragraph #
Step 1. What is the Main Idea:

___

Step 2. List Supporting Details/Examples/Arguments:

___

Step 3. Visualize the Test Question. Convert the Facts into a Test Question: Who? What? When? Where? Why?

___

Paragraph #
Step 1. What is the Main Idea:

___

Step 2. List Supporting Details/Examples/Arguments:

___

Step 3. Visualize the Test Question. Convert the Facts into a Test Question: Who? What? When? Why? Where?

___

SMARTGRADES: NEXT EVOLUTION BRAIN POWER REVOLUTION

Step 4. To Ace the Test, Use Association Cues to Memorize Facts for Instant and Total Recall.

Step 5: Self-Test for Strengths and Weaknesses (Change Weak Association Cues).

List Fact and Memory Association Cue

SMARTGRADES: WE ARE THE FUTURE

Date:
Chapter:
Divide and Conquer: Read One Paragraph at a Time. Number the Paragraphs.
Paragraph #
Step 1. What is the Main Idea:

_____
_____

Step 2. List Supporting Details/Examples/Arguments:

_____
_____
_____
_____
_____
_____

Step 3. Visualize the Test Question. Convert the Facts into a Test Question: Who? What? When? Where? Why?

_____
_____

Paragraph #
Step 1. What is the Main Idea:

_____
_____

Step 2. List Supporting Details/Examples/Arguments:

_____
_____
_____
_____
_____
_____

Step 3. Visualize the Test Question. Convert the Facts into a Test Question: Who? What? When? Why? Where?

_____
_____

SMARTGRADES: NEXT EVOLUTION BRAIN POWER REVOLUTION

Step 4. To Ace the Test, Use Association Cues to Memorize Facts for Instant and Total Recall.

Step 5: Self-Test for Strengths and Weaknesses (Change Weak Association Cues).

List Fact and Memory Association Cue

SMARTGRADES: WE ARE THE FUTURE

Date:
Chapter:
Divide and Conquer: Read One Paragraph at a Time. Number the Paragraphs.
Paragraph #
Step 1. What is the Main Idea:

_____
_____

Step 2. List Supporting Details/Examples/Arguments:

_____
_____
_____
_____
_____
_____

Step 3. Visualize the Test Question. Convert the Facts into a Test Question: Who? What? When? Where? Why?

_____
_____

Paragraph #
Step 1. What is the Main Idea:

_____
_____

Step 2. List Supporting Details/Examples/Arguments:

_____
_____
_____
_____
_____
_____

Step 3. Visualize the Test Question. Convert the Facts into a Test Question: Who? What? When? Why? Where?

_____
_____

SMARTGRADES: NEXT EVOLUTION BRAIN POWER REVOLUTION

Step 4. To Ace the Test, Use Association Cues to Memorize Facts for Instant and Total Recall.

Step 5: Self-Test for Strengths and Weaknesses (Change Weak Association Cues).

List Fact and Memory Association Cue

SMARTGRADES: WE ARE THE FUTURE

Date:
Chapter:
Divide and Conquer: Read One Paragraph at a Time. Number the Paragraphs.
Paragraph #
Step 1. What is the Main Idea:
___
___

Step 2. List Supporting Details/Examples/Arguments:
___
___
___
___
___
___

Step 3. Visualize the Test Question. Convert the Facts into a Test Question: Who? What? When? Where? Why?
___
___

Paragraph #
Step 1. What is the Main Idea:
___
___

Step 2. List Supporting Details/Examples/Arguments:
___
___
___
___
___
___

Step 3. Visualize the Test Question. Convert the Facts into a Test Question: Who? What? When? Why? Where?
___
___

SMARTGRADES: NEXT EVOLUTION BRAIN POWER REVOLUTION

Step 4. To Ace the Test, Use Association Cues to Memorize Facts for Instant and Total Recall.

Step 5: Self-Test for Strengths and Weaknesses (Change Weak Association Cues).

List Fact and Memory Association Cue

SMARTGRADES: WE ARE THE FUTURE

Date:
Chapter:
Divide and Conquer: Read One Paragraph at a Time. Number the Paragraphs.
Paragraph #
Step 1. What is the Main Idea:

_____
_____

Step 2. List Supporting Details/Examples/Arguments:

_____
_____
_____
_____
_____
_____

Step 3. Visualize the Test Question. Convert the Facts into a Test Question: Who? What? When? Where? Why?

_____
_____

Paragraph #
Step 1. What is the Main Idea:

_____
_____

Step 2. List Supporting Details/Examples/Arguments:

_____
_____
_____
_____
_____
_____

Step 3. Visualize the Test Question. Convert the Facts into a Test Question: Who? What? When? Why? Where?

_____
_____

SMARTGRADES: NEXT EVOLUTION BRAIN POWER REVOLUTION

Step 4. To Ace the Test, Use Association Cues to Memorize Facts for Instant and Total Recall.

Step 5: Self-Test for Strengths and Weaknesses (Change Weak Association Cues).

List Fact and Memory Association Cue

SMARTGRADES: WE ARE THE FUTURE

Date:
Chapter:
Divide and Conquer: Read One Paragraph at a Time. Number the Paragraphs.
Paragraph #
Step 1. What is the Main Idea:
_____
_____

Step 2. List Supporting Details/Examples/Arguments:
_____
_____
_____
_____
_____
_____

Step 3. Visualize the Test Question. Convert the Facts into a Test Question: Who? What? When? Where? Why?
_____
_____

Paragraph #
Step 1. What is the Main Idea:
_____
_____

Step 2. List Supporting Details/Examples/Arguments:
_____
_____
_____
_____
_____
_____

Step 3. Visualize the Test Question. Convert the Facts into a Test Question: Who? What? When? Why? Where?
_____
_____

SMARTGRADES: NEXT EVOLUTION BRAIN POWER REVOLUTION

Step 4. To Ace the Test, Use Association Cues to Memorize Facts for Instant and Total Recall.

Step 5: Self-Test for Strengths and Weaknesses (Change Weak Association Cues).

List Fact and Memory Association Cue

SMARTGRADES: WE ARE THE FUTURE

Date:
Chapter:
Divide and Conquer: Read One Paragraph at a Time. Number the Paragraphs.
Paragraph #
Step 1. What is the Main Idea:

_____
_____

Step 2. List Supporting Details/Examples/Arguments:

_____
_____
_____
_____
_____
_____

Step 3. Visualize the Test Question. Convert the Facts into a Test Question: Who? What? When? Where? Why?

_____
_____

Paragraph #
Step 1. What is the Main Idea:

_____
_____

Step 2. List Supporting Details/Examples/Arguments:

_____
_____
_____
_____
_____
_____

Step 3. Visualize the Test Question. Convert the Facts into a Test Question: Who? What? When? Why? Where?

_____
_____

SMARTGRADES: NEXT EVOLUTION BRAIN POWER REVOLUTION

Step 4. To Ace the Test, Use Association Cues to Memorize Facts for Instant and Total Recall.

Step 5: Self-Test for Strengths and Weaknesses (Change Weak Association Cues).

List Fact and Memory Association Cue

SMARTGRADES: WE ARE THE FUTURE

Date:
Chapter:
Divide and Conquer: Read One Paragraph at a Time. Number the Paragraphs.
Paragraph #
Step 1. What is the Main Idea:
_____
_____

Step 2. List Supporting Details/Examples/Arguments:
_____
_____
_____
_____
_____
_____

Step 3. Visualize the Test Question. Convert the Facts into a Test Question: Who? What? When? Where? Why?
_____
_____

Paragraph #
Step 1. What is the Main Idea:
_____
_____

Step 2. List Supporting Details/Examples/Arguments:
_____
_____
_____
_____
_____
_____

Step 3. Visualize the Test Question. Convert the Facts into a Test Question: Who? What? When? Why? Where?
_____
_____

SMARTGRADES: NEXT EVOLUTION BRAIN POWER REVOLUTION

Step 4. To Ace the Test, Use Association Cues to Memorize Facts for Instant and Total Recall.

Step 5: Self-Test for Strengths and Weaknesses (Change Weak Association Cues).

List Fact and Memory Association Cue

SMARTGRADES: WE ARE THE FUTURE

Date:
Chapter:
Divide and Conquer: Read One Paragraph at a Time. Number the Paragraphs.
Paragraph #
Step 1. What is the Main Idea:
_____
_____

Step 2. List Supporting Details/Examples/Arguments:
_____
_____
_____
_____
_____
_____

Step 3. Visualize the Test Question. Convert the Facts into a Test Question: Who? What? When? Where? Why?
_____
_____

Paragraph #
Step 1. What is the Main Idea:
_____
_____

Step 2. List Supporting Details/Examples/Arguments:
_____
_____
_____
_____
_____
_____

Step 3. Visualize the Test Question. Convert the Facts into a Test Question: Who? What? When? Why? Where?
_____
_____

SMARTGRADES: NEXT EVOLUTION BRAIN POWER REVOLUTION

Step 4. To Ace the Test, Use Association Cues to Memorize Facts for Instant and Total Recall.

Step 5: Self-Test for Strengths and Weaknesses (Change Weak Association Cues).

List Fact and Memory Association Cue

SMARTGRADES: WE ARE THE FUTURE

Date:
Chapter:
Divide and Conquer: Read One Paragraph at a Time. Number the Paragraphs.
Paragraph #
Step 1. What is the Main Idea:
_____
_____

Step 2. List Supporting Details/Examples/Arguments:
_____
_____
_____
_____
_____
_____

Step 3. Visualize the Test Question. Convert the Facts into a Test Question: Who? What? When? Where? Why?
_____
_____

Paragraph #
Step 1. What is the Main Idea:
_____
_____

Step 2. List Supporting Details/Examples/Arguments:
_____
_____
_____
_____
_____
_____

Step 3. Visualize the Test Question. Convert the Facts into a Test Question: Who? What? When? Why? Where?
_____
_____

SMARTGRADES: NEXT EVOLUTION BRAIN POWER REVOLUTION

Step 4. To Ace the Test, Use Association Cues to Memorize Facts for Instant and Total Recall.

Step 5: Self-Test for Strengths and Weaknesses (Change Weak Association Cues).

List Fact and Memory Association Cue

SMARTGRADES: WE ARE THE FUTURE

Date:
Chapter:
Divide and Conquer: Read One Paragraph at a Time. Number the Paragraphs.
Paragraph #
Step 1. What is the Main Idea:

_____
_____

Step 2. List Supporting Details/Examples/Arguments:

_____
_____
_____
_____
_____
_____

Step 3. Visualize the Test Question. Convert the Facts into a Test Question: Who? What? When? Where? Why?

_____
_____

Paragraph #
Step 1. What is the Main Idea:

_____
_____

Step 2. List Supporting Details/Examples/Arguments:

_____
_____
_____
_____
_____
_____

Step 3. Visualize the Test Question. Convert the Facts into a Test Question: Who? What? When? Why? Where?

_____
_____

SMARTGRADES: NEXT EVOLUTION BRAIN POWER REVOLUTION

Step 4. To Ace the Test, Use Association Cues to Memorize Facts for Instant and Total Recall.

Step 5: Self-Test for Strengths and Weaknesses (Change Weak Association Cues).

List Fact and Memory Association Cue

SMARTGRADES: WE ARE THE FUTURE

Date:
Chapter:
Divide and Conquer: Read One Paragraph at a Time. Number the Paragraphs.
Paragraph #
Step 1. What is the Main Idea:
_____
_____

Step 2. List Supporting Details/Examples/Arguments:
_____
_____
_____
_____
_____
_____

Step 3. Visualize the Test Question. Convert the Facts into a Test Question: Who? What? When? Where? Why?
_____
_____

Paragraph #
Step 1. What is the Main Idea:
_____
_____

Step 2. List Supporting Details/Examples/Arguments:
_____
_____
_____
_____
_____
_____

Step 3. Visualize the Test Question. Convert the Facts into a Test Question: Who? What? When? Why? Where?
_____
_____

SMARTGRADES: NEXT EVOLUTION BRAIN POWER REVOLUTION

Step 4. To Ace the Test, Use Association Cues to Memorize Facts for Instant and Total Recall.

Step 5: Self-Test for Strengths and Weaknesses (Change Weak Association Cues).

List Fact and Memory Association Cue

SMARTGRADES: WE ARE THE FUTURE

Date:
Chapter:
Divide and Conquer: Read One Paragraph at a Time. Number the Paragraphs.
Paragraph #
Step 1. What is the Main Idea:

_____
_____

Step 2. List Supporting Details/Examples/Arguments:

_____
_____
_____
_____
_____
_____

Step 3. Visualize the Test Question. Convert the Facts into a Test Question: Who? What? When? Where? Why?

_____
_____

Paragraph #
Step 1. What is the Main Idea:

_____
_____

Step 2. List Supporting Details/Examples/Arguments:

_____
_____
_____
_____
_____
_____

Step 3. Visualize the Test Question. Convert the Facts into a Test Question: Who? What? When? Why? Where?

_____
_____

SMARTGRADES: NEXT EVOLUTION BRAIN POWER REVOLUTION

Step 4. To Ace the Test, Use Association Cues to Memorize Facts for Instant and Total Recall.

Step 5: Self-Test for Strengths and Weaknesses (Change Weak Association Cues).

List Fact and Memory Association Cue

SMARTGRADES: WE ARE THE FUTURE

Date:
Chapter:
Divide and Conquer: Read One Paragraph at a Time. Number the Paragraphs.
Paragraph #
Step 1. What is the Main Idea:

_____
_____

Step 2. List Supporting Details/Examples/Arguments:

_____
_____
_____
_____
_____
_____

Step 3. Visualize the Test Question. Convert the Facts into a Test Question: Who? What? When? Where? Why?

_____
_____

Paragraph #
Step 1. What is the Main Idea:

_____
_____

Step 2. List Supporting Details/Examples/Arguments:

_____
_____
_____
_____
_____
_____

Step 3. Visualize the Test Question. Convert the Facts into a Test Question: Who? What? When? Why? Where?

_____
_____

SMARTGRADES: NEXT EVOLUTION BRAIN POWER REVOLUTION

Step 4. To Ace the Test, Use Association Cues to Memorize Facts for Instant and Total Recall.

Step 5: Self-Test for Strengths and Weaknesses (Change Weak Association Cues).

List Fact and Memory Association Cue

SMARTGRADES: WE ARE THE FUTURE

Date:
Chapter:
Divide and Conquer: Read One Paragraph at a Time. Number the Paragraphs.
Paragraph #
Step 1. What is the Main Idea:

_____
_____

Step 2. List Supporting Details/Examples/Arguments:

_____
_____
_____
_____
_____
_____

Step 3. Visualize the Test Question. Convert the Facts into a Test Question: Who? What? When? Where? Why?

_____
_____

Paragraph #
Step 1. What is the Main Idea:

_____
_____

Step 2. List Supporting Details/Examples/Arguments:

_____
_____
_____
_____
_____
_____

Step 3. Visualize the Test Question. Convert the Facts into a Test Question: Who? What? When? Why? Where?

_____
_____

SMARTGRADES: NEXT EVOLUTION BRAIN POWER REVOLUTION

Step 4. To Ace the Test, Use Association Cues to Memorize Facts for Instant and Total Recall.

Step 5: Self-Test for Strengths and Weaknesses (Change Weak Association Cues).

List Fact and Memory Association Cue

SMARTGRADES: WE ARE THE FUTURE

Date:
Chapter:
Divide and Conquer: Read One Paragraph at a Time. Number the Paragraphs.
Paragraph #
Step 1. What is the Main Idea:

_____
_____

Step 2. List Supporting Details/Examples/Arguments:

_____
_____
_____
_____
_____
_____

Step 3. Visualize the Test Question. Convert the Facts into a Test Question: Who? What? When? Where? Why?

_____
_____

Paragraph #
Step 1. What is the Main Idea:

_____
_____

Step 2. List Supporting Details/Examples/Arguments:

_____
_____
_____
_____
_____
_____

Step 3. Visualize the Test Question. Convert the Facts into a Test Question: Who? What? When? Why? Where?

_____
_____

SMARTGRADES: NEXT EVOLUTION BRAIN POWER REVOLUTION

Step 4. To Ace the Test, Use Association Cues to Memorize Facts for Instant and Total Recall.

Step 5: Self-Test for Strengths and Weaknesses (Change Weak Association Cues).

List Fact and Memory Association Cue

SMARTGRADES: WE ARE THE FUTURE

Date:
Chapter:
Divide and Conquer: Read One Paragraph at a Time. Number the Paragraphs.
Paragraph #
Step 1. What is the Main Idea:

_____
_____

Step 2. List Supporting Details/Examples/Arguments:

_____
_____
_____
_____
_____
_____

Step 3. Visualize the Test Question. Convert the Facts into a Test Question: Who? What? When? Where? Why?

_____
_____

Paragraph #
Step 1. What is the Main Idea:

_____
_____

Step 2. List Supporting Details/Examples/Arguments:

_____
_____
_____
_____
_____
_____

Step 3. Visualize the Test Question. Convert the Facts into a Test Question: Who? What? When? Why? Where?

_____
_____

SMARTGRADES: NEXT EVOLUTION BRAIN POWER REVOLUTION

Step 4. To Ace the Test, Use Association Cues to Memorize Facts for Instant and Total Recall.

Step 5: Self-Test for Strengths and Weaknesses (Change Weak Association Cues).

List Fact and Memory Association Cue

SMARTGRADES: WE ARE THE FUTURE

Date:
Chapter:
Divide and Conquer: Read One Paragraph at a Time. Number the Paragraphs.
Paragraph #
Step 1. What is the Main Idea:

_____
_____

Step 2. List Supporting Details/Examples/Arguments:

_____
_____
_____
_____
_____
_____

Step 3. Visualize the Test Question. Convert the Facts into a Test Question: Who? What? When? Where? Why?

_____
_____

Paragraph #
Step 1. What is the Main Idea:

_____
_____

Step 2. List Supporting Details/Examples/Arguments:

_____
_____
_____
_____
_____
_____

Step 3. Visualize the Test Question. Convert the Facts into a Test Question: Who? What? When? Why? Where?

_____
_____

SMARTGRADES: NEXT EVOLUTION BRAIN POWER REVOLUTION

Step 4. To Ace the Test, Use Association Cues to Memorize Facts for Instant and Total Recall.

Step 5: Self-Test for Strengths and Weaknesses (Change Weak Association Cues).

List Fact and Memory Association Cue

SMARTGRADES: WE ARE THE FUTURE

Date:
Chapter:
Divide and Conquer: Read One Paragraph at a Time. Number the Paragraphs.
Paragraph #
Step 1. What is the Main Idea:

_____
_____

Step 2. List Supporting Details/Examples/Arguments:

_____
_____
_____
_____
_____
_____

Step 3. Visualize the Test Question. Convert the Facts into a Test Question: Who? What? When? Where? Why?

_____
_____

Paragraph #
Step 1. What is the Main Idea:

_____
_____

Step 2. List Supporting Details/Examples/Arguments:

_____
_____
_____
_____
_____
_____

Step 3. Visualize the Test Question. Convert the Facts into a Test Question: Who? What? When? Why? Where?

_____
_____

SMARTGRADES: NEXT EVOLUTION BRAIN POWER REVOLUTION

Step 4. To Ace the Test, Use Association Cues to Memorize Facts for Instant and Total Recall.

Step 5: Self-Test for Strengths and Weaknesses (Change Weak Association Cues).

List Fact and Memory Association Cue

SMARTGRADES: WE ARE THE FUTURE

Date:
Chapter:
Divide and Conquer: Read One Paragraph at a Time. Number the Paragraphs.
Paragraph #
Step 1. What is the Main Idea:

_____
_____

Step 2. List Supporting Details/Examples/Arguments:

_____
_____
_____
_____
_____
_____

Step 3. Visualize the Test Question. Convert the Facts into a Test Question: Who? What? When? Where? Why?

_____
_____

Paragraph #
Step 1. What is the Main Idea:

_____
_____

Step 2. List Supporting Details/Examples/Arguments:

_____
_____
_____
_____
_____
_____

Step 3. Visualize the Test Question. Convert the Facts into a Test Question: Who? What? When? Why? Where?

_____
_____

SMARTGRADES: NEXT EVOLUTION BRAIN POWER REVOLUTION

Step 4. To Ace the Test, Use Association Cues to Memorize Facts for Instant and Total Recall.

Step 5: Self-Test for Strengths and Weaknesses (Change Weak Association Cues).

List Fact and Memory Association Cue

SMARTGRADES: WE ARE THE FUTURE

Date:
Chapter:
Divide and Conquer: Read One Paragraph at a Time. Number the Paragraphs.
Paragraph #
Step 1. What is the Main Idea:

_____
_____

Step 2. List Supporting Details/Examples/Arguments:

_____
_____
_____
_____
_____
_____

Step 3. Visualize the Test Question. Convert the Facts into a Test Question: Who? What? When? Where? Why?

_____
_____

Paragraph #
Step 1. What is the Main Idea:

_____
_____

Step 2. List Supporting Details/Examples/Arguments:

_____
_____
_____
_____
_____
_____

Step 3. Visualize the Test Question. Convert the Facts into a Test Question: Who? What? When? Why? Where?

_____
_____

SMARTGRADES: NEXT EVOLUTION BRAIN POWER REVOLUTION

Step 4. To Ace the Test, Use Association Cues to Memorize Facts for Instant and Total Recall.

Step 5: Self-Test for Strengths and Weaknesses (Change Weak Association Cues).

List Fact and Memory Association Cue

SMARTGRADES: WE ARE THE FUTURE

Date:
Chapter:
Divide and Conquer: Read One Paragraph at a Time. Number the Paragraphs.
Paragraph #
Step 1. What is the Main Idea:

___
___

Step 2. List Supporting Details/Examples/Arguments:

___
___
___
___
___
___

Step 3. Visualize the Test Question. Convert the Facts into a Test Question: Who? What? When? Where? Why?

___
___

Paragraph #
Step 1. What is the Main Idea:

___
___

Step 2. List Supporting Details/Examples/Arguments:

___
___
___
___
___
___

Step 3. Visualize the Test Question. Convert the Facts into a Test Question: Who? What? When? Why? Where?

___
___

SMARTGRADES: NEXT EVOLUTION BRAIN POWER REVOLUTION

Step 4. To Ace the Test, Use Association Cues to Memorize Facts for Instant and Total Recall.

Step 5: Self-Test for Strengths and Weaknesses (Change Weak Association Cues).

List Fact and Memory Association Cue

SMARTGRADES: WE ARE THE FUTURE

Date:
Chapter:
Divide and Conquer: Read One Paragraph at a Time. Number the Paragraphs.
Paragraph #
Step 1. What is the Main Idea:

_____
_____

Step 2. List Supporting Details/Examples/Arguments:

_____
_____
_____
_____
_____
_____

Step 3. Visualize the Test Question. Convert the Facts into a Test Question: Who? What? When? Where? Why?

_____
_____

Paragraph #
Step 1. What is the Main Idea:

_____
_____

Step 2. List Supporting Details/Examples/Arguments:

_____
_____
_____
_____
_____
_____

Step 3. Visualize the Test Question. Convert the Facts into a Test Question: Who? What? When? Why? Where?

_____
_____

SMARTGRADES: NEXT EVOLUTION BRAIN POWER REVOLUTION

Step 4. To Ace the Test, Use Association Cues to Memorize Facts for Instant and Total Recall.

Step 5: Self-Test for Strengths and Weaknesses (Change Weak Association Cues).

List Fact and Memory Association Cue

SMARTGRADES: WE ARE THE FUTURE

Date:
Chapter:
Divide and Conquer: Read One Paragraph at a Time. Number the Paragraphs.
Paragraph #
Step 1. What is the Main Idea:

_____
_____

Step 2. List Supporting Details/Examples/Arguments:

_____
_____
_____
_____
_____
_____

Step 3. Visualize the Test Question. Convert the Facts into a Test Question: Who? What? When? Where? Why?

_____
_____

Paragraph #
Step 1. What is the Main Idea:

_____
_____

Step 2. List Supporting Details/Examples/Arguments:

_____
_____
_____
_____
_____
_____

Step 3. Visualize the Test Question. Convert the Facts into a Test Question: Who? What? When? Why? Where?

_____
_____

SMARTGRADES: NEXT EVOLUTION BRAIN POWER REVOLUTION

Step 4. To Ace the Test, Use Association Cues to Memorize Facts for Instant and Total Recall.

Step 5: Self-Test for Strengths and Weaknesses (Change Weak Association Cues).

List Fact and Memory Association Cue

SMARTGRADES: WE ARE THE FUTURE

Date:
Chapter:
Divide and Conquer: Read One Paragraph at a Time. Number the Paragraphs.
Paragraph #
Step 1. What is the Main Idea:

_____
_____

Step 2. List Supporting Details/Examples/Arguments:

_____
_____
_____
_____
_____
_____

Step 3. Visualize the Test Question. Convert the Facts into a Test Question: Who? What? When? Where? Why?

_____
_____

Paragraph #
Step 1. What is the Main Idea:

_____
_____

Step 2. List Supporting Details/Examples/Arguments:

_____
_____
_____
_____
_____
_____

Step 3. Visualize the Test Question. Convert the Facts into a Test Question: Who? What? When? Why? Where?

_____
_____

SMARTGRADES: NEXT EVOLUTION BRAIN POWER REVOLUTION

Step 4. To Ace the Test, Use Association Cues to Memorize Facts for Instant and Total Recall.

Step 5: Self-Test for Strengths and Weaknesses (Change Weak Association Cues).

List Fact and Memory Association Cue

SMARTGRADES: WE ARE THE FUTURE

Date:
Chapter:
Divide and Conquer: Read One Paragraph at a Time. Number the Paragraphs.
Paragraph #
Step 1. What is the Main Idea:
_____
_____

Step 2. List Supporting Details/Examples/Arguments:
_____
_____
_____
_____
_____
_____

Step 3. Visualize the Test Question. Convert the Facts into a Test Question: Who? What? When? Where? Why?
_____
_____

Paragraph #
Step 1. What is the Main Idea:
_____
_____

Step 2. List Supporting Details/Examples/Arguments:
_____
_____
_____
_____
_____
_____

Step 3. Visualize the Test Question. Convert the Facts into a Test Question: Who? What? When? Why? Where?
_____
_____

SMARTGRADES: NEXT EVOLUTION BRAIN POWER REVOLUTION

Step 4. To Ace the Test, Use Association Cues to Memorize Facts for Instant and Total Recall.

Step 5: Self-Test for Strengths and Weaknesses (Change Weak Association Cues).

List Fact and Memory Association Cue

SMARTGRADES: WE ARE THE FUTURE

Date:
Chapter:
Divide and Conquer: Read One Paragraph at a Time. Number the Paragraphs.
Paragraph #
Step 1. What is the Main Idea:

_____
_____

Step 2. List Supporting Details/Examples/Arguments:

_____
_____
_____
_____
_____
_____

Step 3. Visualize the Test Question. Convert the Facts into a Test Question: Who? What? When? Where? Why?

_____
_____

Paragraph #
Step 1. What is the Main Idea:

_____
_____

Step 2. List Supporting Details/Examples/Arguments:

_____
_____
_____
_____
_____
_____

Step 3. Visualize the Test Question. Convert the Facts into a Test Question: Who? What? When? Why? Where?

_____
_____

SMARTGRADES: NEXT EVOLUTION BRAIN POWER REVOLUTION

Step 4. To Ace the Test, Use Association Cues to Memorize Facts for Instant and Total Recall.

Step 5: Self-Test for Strengths and Weaknesses (Change Weak Association Cues).

List Fact and Memory Association Cue

SMARTGRADES: WE ARE THE FUTURE

Date:
Chapter:
Divide and Conquer: Read One Paragraph at a Time. Number the Paragraphs.
Paragraph #
Step 1. What is the Main Idea:
_____
_____

Step 2. List Supporting Details/Examples/Arguments:
_____
_____
_____
_____
_____
_____

Step 3. Visualize the Test Question. Convert the Facts into a Test Question: Who? What? When? Where? Why?
_____
_____

Paragraph #
Step 1. What is the Main Idea:
_____
_____

Step 2. List Supporting Details/Examples/Arguments:
_____
_____
_____
_____
_____
_____

Step 3. Visualize the Test Question. Convert the Facts into a Test Question: Who? What? When? Why? Where?
_____
_____

SMARTGRADES: NEXT EVOLUTION BRAIN POWER REVOLUTION

Step 4. To Ace the Test, Use Association Cues to Memorize Facts for Instant and Total Recall.

Step 5: Self-Test for Strengths and Weaknesses (Change Weak Association Cues).

List Fact and Memory Association Cue

SMARTGRADES: WE ARE THE FUTURE

Date:
Chapter:
Divide and Conquer: Read One Paragraph at a Time. Number the Paragraphs.
Paragraph #
Step 1. What is the Main Idea:

_____
_____

Step 2. List Supporting Details/Examples/Arguments:

_____
_____
_____
_____
_____
_____

Step 3. Visualize the Test Question. Convert the Facts into a Test Question: Who? What? When? Where? Why?

_____
_____

Paragraph #
Step 1. What is the Main Idea:

_____
_____

Step 2. List Supporting Details/Examples/Arguments:

_____
_____
_____
_____
_____
_____

Step 3. Visualize the Test Question. Convert the Facts into a Test Question: Who? What? When? Why? Where?

_____
_____

SMARTGRADES: NEXT EVOLUTION BRAIN POWER REVOLUTION

Step 4. To Ace the Test, Use Association Cues to Memorize Facts for Instant and Total Recall.

Step 5: Self-Test for Strengths and Weaknesses (Change Weak Association Cues).

List Fact and Memory Association Cue

SMARTGRADES: WE ARE THE FUTURE

Date:
Chapter:
Divide and Conquer: Read One Paragraph at a Time. Number the Paragraphs.
Paragraph #
Step 1. What is the Main Idea:

_____
_____

Step 2. List Supporting Details/Examples/Arguments:

_____
_____
_____
_____
_____
_____

Step 3. Visualize the Test Question. Convert the Facts into a Test Question: Who? What? When? Where? Why?

_____
_____

Paragraph #
Step 1. What is the Main Idea:

_____
_____

Step 2. List Supporting Details/Examples/Arguments:

_____
_____
_____
_____
_____
_____

Step 3. Visualize the Test Question. Convert the Facts into a Test Question: Who? What? When? Why? Where?

_____
_____

SMARTGRADES: NEXT EVOLUTION BRAIN POWER REVOLUTION

Step 4. To Ace the Test, Use Association Cues to Memorize Facts for Instant and Total Recall.

Step 5: Self-Test for Strengths and Weaknesses (Change Weak Association Cues).

List Fact and Memory Association Cue

SMARTGRADES: WE ARE THE FUTURE

Date:
Chapter:
Divide and Conquer: Read One Paragraph at a Time. Number the Paragraphs.
Paragraph #
Step 1. What is the Main Idea:

_____
_____

Step 2. List Supporting Details/Examples/Arguments:

_____
_____
_____
_____
_____
_____

Step 3. Visualize the Test Question. Convert the Facts into a Test Question: Who? What? When? Where? Why?

_____
_____

Paragraph #
Step 1. What is the Main Idea:

_____
_____

Step 2. List Supporting Details/Examples/Arguments:

_____
_____
_____
_____
_____
_____

Step 3. Visualize the Test Question. Convert the Facts into a Test Question: Who? What? When? Why? Where?

_____
_____

SMARTGRADES: NEXT EVOLUTION BRAIN POWER REVOLUTION

Step 4. To Ace the Test, Use Association Cues to Memorize Facts for Instant and Total Recall.

Step 5: Self-Test for Strengths and Weaknesses (Change Weak Association Cues).

List Fact and Memory Association Cue

SMARTGRADES: WE ARE THE FUTURE

Date:
Chapter:
Divide and Conquer: Read One Paragraph at a Time. Number the Paragraphs.
Paragraph #
Step 1. What is the Main Idea:
_____
_____

Step 2. List Supporting Details/Examples/Arguments:
_____
_____
_____
_____
_____
_____

Step 3. Visualize the Test Question. Convert the Facts into a Test Question: Who? What? When? Where? Why?
_____
_____

Paragraph #
Step 1. What is the Main Idea:
_____
_____

Step 2. List Supporting Details/Examples/Arguments:
_____
_____
_____
_____
_____
_____

Step 3. Visualize the Test Question. Convert the Facts into a Test Question: Who? What? When? Why? Where?
_____
_____

SMARTGRADES: NEXT EVOLUTION BRAIN POWER REVOLUTION

Step 4. To Ace the Test, Use Association Cues to Memorize Facts for Instant and Total Recall.

Step 5: Self-Test for Strengths and Weaknesses (Change Weak Association Cues).

List Fact and Memory Association Cue

SMARTGRADES: WE ARE THE FUTURE

Date:
Chapter:
Divide and Conquer: Read One Paragraph at a Time. Number the Paragraphs.
Paragraph #
Step 1. What is the Main Idea:

_____
_____

Step 2. List Supporting Details/Examples/Arguments:

_____
_____
_____
_____
_____
_____

Step 3. Visualize the Test Question. Convert the Facts into a Test Question: Who? What? When? Where? Why?

_____
_____

Paragraph #
Step 1. What is the Main Idea:

_____
_____

Step 2. List Supporting Details/Examples/Arguments:

_____
_____
_____
_____
_____
_____

Step 3. Visualize the Test Question. Convert the Facts into a Test Question: Who? What? When? Why? Where?

_____
_____

SMARTGRADES: NEXT EVOLUTION BRAIN POWER REVOLUTION

Step 4. To Ace the Test, Use Association Cues to Memorize Facts for Instant and Total Recall.

Step 5: Self-Test for Strengths and Weaknesses (Change Weak Association Cues).

List Fact and Memory Association Cue

SMARTGRADES: WE ARE THE FUTURE

Date:
Chapter:
Divide and Conquer: Read One Paragraph at a Time. Number the Paragraphs.
Paragraph #
Step 1. What is the Main Idea:

_____
_____

Step 2. List Supporting Details/Examples/Arguments:

_____
_____
_____
_____
_____
_____

Step 3. Visualize the Test Question. Convert the Facts into a Test Question: Who? What? When? Where? Why?

_____
_____

Paragraph #
Step 1. What is the Main Idea:

_____
_____

Step 2. List Supporting Details/Examples/Arguments:

_____
_____
_____
_____
_____
_____

Step 3. Visualize the Test Question. Convert the Facts into a Test Question: Who? What? When? Why? Where?

_____
_____

SMARTGRADES: NEXT EVOLUTION BRAIN POWER REVOLUTION

Step 4. To Ace the Test, Use Association Cues to Memorize Facts for Instant and Total Recall.

Step 5: Self-Test for Strengths and Weaknesses (Change Weak Association Cues).

List Fact and Memory Association Cue

SMARTGRADES: WE ARE THE FUTURE

Date:
Chapter:
Divide and Conquer: Read One Paragraph at a Time. Number the Paragraphs.
Paragraph #
Step 1. What is the Main Idea:

_____
_____

Step 2. List Supporting Details/Examples/Arguments:

_____
_____
_____
_____
_____
_____

Step 3. Visualize the Test Question. Convert the Facts into a Test Question: Who? What? When? Where? Why?

_____
_____

Paragraph #
Step 1. What is the Main Idea:

_____
_____

Step 2. List Supporting Details/Examples/Arguments:

_____
_____
_____
_____
_____
_____

Step 3. Visualize the Test Question. Convert the Facts into a Test Question: Who? What? When? Why? Where?

_____
_____

SMARTGRADES: NEXT EVOLUTION BRAIN POWER REVOLUTION

Step 4. To Ace the Test, Use Association Cues to Memorize Facts for Instant and Total Recall.

Step 5: Self-Test for Strengths and Weaknesses (Change Weak Association Cues).

List Fact and Memory Association Cue

SMARTGRADES: WE ARE THE FUTURE

Date:
Chapter:
Divide and Conquer: Read One Paragraph at a Time. Number the Paragraphs.
Paragraph #
Step 1. What is the Main Idea:

_____
_____

Step 2. List Supporting Details/Examples/Arguments:

_____
_____
_____
_____
_____
_____

Step 3. Visualize the Test Question. Convert the Facts into a Test Question: Who? What? When? Where? Why?

_____
_____

Paragraph #
Step 1. What is the Main Idea:

_____
_____

Step 2. List Supporting Details/Examples/Arguments:

_____
_____
_____
_____
_____
_____

Step 3. Visualize the Test Question. Convert the Facts into a Test Question: Who? What? When? Why? Where?

_____
_____

SMARTGRADES: NEXT EVOLUTION BRAIN POWER REVOLUTION

Step 4. To Ace the Test, Use Association Cues to Memorize Facts for Instant and Total Recall.

Step 5: Self-Test for Strengths and Weaknesses (Change Weak Association Cues).

List Fact and Memory Association Cue

SMARTGRADES: WE ARE THE FUTURE

Date:
Chapter:
Divide and Conquer: Read One Paragraph at a Time. Number the Paragraphs.
Paragraph #
Step 1. What is the Main Idea:

_____
_____

Step 2. List Supporting Details/Examples/Arguments:

_____
_____
_____
_____
_____
_____

Step 3. Visualize the Test Question. Convert the Facts into a Test Question: Who? What? When? Where? Why?

_____
_____

Paragraph #
Step 1. What is the Main Idea:

_____
_____

Step 2. List Supporting Details/Examples/Arguments:

_____
_____
_____
_____
_____
_____

Step 3. Visualize the Test Question. Convert the Facts into a Test Question: Who? What? When? Why? Where?

_____
_____

SMARTGRADES: NEXT EVOLUTION BRAIN POWER REVOLUTION

Step 4. To Ace the Test, Use Association Cues to Memorize Facts for Instant and Total Recall.

Step 5: Self-Test for Strengths and Weaknesses (Change Weak Association Cues).

List Fact and Memory Association Cue

SMARTGRADES: WE ARE THE FUTURE

Date:
Chapter:
Divide and Conquer: Read One Paragraph at a Time. Number the Paragraphs.
Paragraph #
Step 1. What is the Main Idea:

_____
_____

Step 2. List Supporting Details/Examples/Arguments:

_____
_____
_____
_____
_____
_____

Step 3. Visualize the Test Question. Convert the Facts into a Test Question: Who? What? When? Where? Why?

_____
_____

Paragraph #
Step 1. What is the Main Idea:

_____
_____

Step 2. List Supporting Details/Examples/Arguments:

_____
_____
_____
_____
_____
_____

Step 3. Visualize the Test Question. Convert the Facts into a Test Question: Who? What? When? Why? Where?

_____
_____

SMARTGRADES: NEXT EVOLUTION BRAIN POWER REVOLUTION

Step 4. To Ace the Test, Use Association Cues to Memorize Facts for Instant and Total Recall.

Step 5: Self-Test for Strengths and Weaknesses (Change Weak Association Cues).

List Fact and Memory Association Cue

SMARTGRADES: WE ARE THE FUTURE

Date:
Chapter:
Divide and Conquer: Read One Paragraph at a Time. Number the Paragraphs.
Paragraph #
Step 1. What is the Main Idea:

_____
_____

Step 2. List Supporting Details/Examples/Arguments:

_____
_____
_____
_____
_____
_____

Step 3. Visualize the Test Question. Convert the Facts into a Test Question: Who? What? When? Where? Why?

_____
_____

Paragraph #
Step 1. What is the Main Idea:

_____
_____

Step 2. List Supporting Details/Examples/Arguments:

_____
_____
_____
_____
_____
_____

Step 3. Visualize the Test Question. Convert the Facts into a Test Question: Who? What? When? Why? Where?

_____
_____

SMARTGRADES: NEXT EVOLUTION BRAIN POWER REVOLUTION

Step 4. To Ace the Test, Use Association Cues to Memorize Facts for Instant and Total Recall.

Step 5: Self-Test for Strengths and Weaknesses (Change Weak Association Cues).

List Fact and Memory Association Cue

SMARTGRADES: WE ARE THE FUTURE

Date:
Chapter:
Divide and Conquer: Read One Paragraph at a Time. Number the Paragraphs.
Paragraph #
Step 1. What is the Main Idea:

_____
_____

Step 2. List Supporting Details/Examples/Arguments:

_____
_____
_____
_____
_____
_____

Step 3. Visualize the Test Question. Convert the Facts into a Test Question: Who? What? When? Where? Why?

_____
_____

Paragraph #
Step 1. What is the Main Idea:

_____
_____

Step 2. List Supporting Details/Examples/Arguments:

_____
_____
_____
_____
_____
_____

Step 3. Visualize the Test Question. Convert the Facts into a Test Question: Who? What? When? Why? Where?

_____
_____

SMARTGRADES: NEXT EVOLUTION BRAIN POWER REVOLUTION

Step 4. To Ace the Test, Use Association Cues to Memorize Facts for Instant and Total Recall.

Step 5: Self-Test for Strengths and Weaknesses (Change Weak Association Cues).

                              List Fact and Memory Association Cue

SMARTGRADES: WE ARE THE FUTURE

Date:
Chapter:
Divide and Conquer: Read One Paragraph at a Time. Number the Paragraphs.
Paragraph #
Step 1. What is the Main Idea:

_____
_____

Step 2. List Supporting Details/Examples/Arguments:

_____
_____
_____
_____
_____
_____

Step 3. Visualize the Test Question. Convert the Facts into a Test Question: Who? What? When? Where? Why?

_____
_____

Paragraph #
Step 1. What is the Main Idea:

_____
_____

Step 2. List Supporting Details/Examples/Arguments:

_____
_____
_____
_____
_____
_____

Step 3. Visualize the Test Question. Convert the Facts into a Test Question: Who? What? When? Why? Where?

_____
_____

SMARTGRADES: NEXT EVOLUTION BRAIN POWER REVOLUTION

Step 4. To Ace the Test, Use Association Cues to Memorize Facts for Instant and Total Recall.

Step 5: Self-Test for Strengths and Weaknesses (Change Weak Association Cues).

List Fact and Memory Association Cue

SMARTGRADES: WE ARE THE FUTURE

Date:
Chapter:
Divide and Conquer: Read One Paragraph at a Time. Number the Paragraphs.
Paragraph #
Step 1. What is the Main Idea:

_____
_____

Step 2. List Supporting Details/Examples/Arguments:

_____
_____
_____
_____
_____
_____

Step 3. Visualize the Test Question. Convert the Facts into a Test Question: Who? What? When? Where? Why?

_____
_____

Paragraph #
Step 1. What is the Main Idea:

_____
_____

Step 2. List Supporting Details/Examples/Arguments:

_____
_____
_____
_____
_____
_____

Step 3. Visualize the Test Question. Convert the Facts into a Test Question: Who? What? When? Why? Where?

_____
_____

SMARTGRADES: NEXT EVOLUTION BRAIN POWER REVOLUTION

Step 4. To Ace the Test, Use Association Cues to Memorize Facts for Instant and Total Recall.

Step 5: Self-Test for Strengths and Weaknesses (Change Weak Association Cues).

List Fact and Memory Association Cue

SMARTGRADES: WE ARE THE FUTURE

Date:
Chapter:
Divide and Conquer: Read One Paragraph at a Time. Number the Paragraphs.
Paragraph #
Step 1. What is the Main Idea:

_____
_____

Step 2. List Supporting Details/Examples/Arguments:

_____
_____
_____
_____
_____
_____

Step 3. Visualize the Test Question. Convert the Facts into a Test Question: Who? What? When? Where? Why?

_____
_____

Paragraph #
Step 1. What is the Main Idea:

_____
_____

Step 2. List Supporting Details/Examples/Arguments:

_____
_____
_____
_____
_____
_____

Step 3. Visualize the Test Question. Convert the Facts into a Test Question: Who? What? When? Why? Where?

_____
_____

SMARTGRADES: NEXT EVOLUTION BRAIN POWER REVOLUTION

Step 4. To Ace the Test, Use Association Cues to Memorize Facts for Instant and Total Recall.

Step 5: Self-Test for Strengths and Weaknesses (Change Weak Association Cues).

List Fact and Memory Association Cue

SMARTGRADES: WE ARE THE FUTURE

Date:
Chapter:
Divide and Conquer: Read One Paragraph at a Time. Number the Paragraphs.
Paragraph #
Step 1. What is the Main Idea:

_____
_____

Step 2. List Supporting Details/Examples/Arguments:

_____
_____
_____
_____
_____
_____

Step 3. Visualize the Test Question. Convert the Facts into a Test Question: Who? What? When? Where? Why?

_____
_____

Paragraph #
Step 1. What is the Main Idea:

_____
_____

Step 2. List Supporting Details/Examples/Arguments:

_____
_____
_____
_____
_____
_____

Step 3. Visualize the Test Question. Convert the Facts into a Test Question: Who? What? When? Why? Where?

_____
_____

SMARTGRADES: NEXT EVOLUTION BRAIN POWER REVOLUTION

Step 4. To Ace the Test, Use Association Cues to Memorize Facts for Instant and Total Recall.

Step 5: Self-Test for Strengths and Weaknesses (Change Weak Association Cues).

List Fact and Memory Association Cue

SMARTGRADES: WE ARE THE FUTURE

Date:
Chapter:
Divide and Conquer: Read One Paragraph at a Time. Number the Paragraphs.
Paragraph #
Step 1. What is the Main Idea:

_____
_____

Step 2. List Supporting Details/Examples/Arguments:

_____
_____
_____
_____
_____
_____

Step 3. Visualize the Test Question. Convert the Facts into a Test Question: Who? What? When? Where? Why?

_____
_____

Paragraph #
Step 1. What is the Main Idea:

_____
_____

Step 2. List Supporting Details/Examples/Arguments:

_____
_____
_____
_____
_____
_____

Step 3. Visualize the Test Question. Convert the Facts into a Test Question: Who? What? When? Why? Where?

_____
_____

SMARTGRADES: NEXT EVOLUTION BRAIN POWER REVOLUTION

Step 4. To Ace the Test, Use Association Cues to Memorize Facts for Instant and Total Recall.

Step 5: Self-Test for Strengths and Weaknesses (Change Weak Association Cues).

List Fact and Memory Association Cue

SMARTGRADES: WE ARE THE FUTURE

Date:
Chapter:
Divide and Conquer: Read One Paragraph at a Time. Number the Paragraphs.
Paragraph #
Step 1. What is the Main Idea:

___

Step 2. List Supporting Details/Examples/Arguments:

___

Step 3. Visualize the Test Question. Convert the Facts into a Test Question: Who? What? When? Where? Why?

___

Paragraph #
Step 1. What is the Main Idea:

___

Step 2. List Supporting Details/Examples/Arguments:

___

Step 3. Visualize the Test Question. Convert the Facts into a Test Question: Who? What? When? Why? Where?

___

SMARTGRADES: NEXT EVOLUTION BRAIN POWER REVOLUTION

Step 4. To Ace the Test, Use Association Cues to Memorize Facts for Instant and Total Recall.

Step 5: Self-Test for Strengths and Weaknesses (Change Weak Association Cues).

List Fact and Memory Association Cue

SMARTGRADES: WE ARE THE FUTURE

Date:
Chapter:
Divide and Conquer: Read One Paragraph at a Time. Number the Paragraphs.
Paragraph #
Step 1. What is the Main Idea:

_____
_____

Step 2. List Supporting Details/Examples/Arguments:

_____
_____
_____
_____
_____
_____

Step 3. Visualize the Test Question. Convert the Facts into a Test Question: Who? What? When? Where? Why?

_____
_____

Paragraph #
Step 1. What is the Main Idea:

_____
_____

Step 2. List Supporting Details/Examples/Arguments:

_____
_____
_____
_____
_____
_____

Step 3. Visualize the Test Question. Convert the Facts into a Test Question: Who? What? When? Why? Where?

_____
_____

SMARTGRADES: NEXT EVOLUTION BRAIN POWER REVOLUTION

Step 4. To Ace the Test, Use Association Cues to Memorize Facts for Instant and Total Recall.

Step 5: Self-Test for Strengths and Weaknesses (Change Weak Association Cues).

List Fact and Memory Association Cue

SMARTGRADES: WE ARE THE FUTURE

Date:
Chapter:
Divide and Conquer: Read One Paragraph at a Time. Number the Paragraphs.
Paragraph #
Step 1. What is the Main Idea:

_____
_____

Step 2. List Supporting Details/Examples/Arguments:

_____
_____
_____
_____
_____
_____

Step 3. Visualize the Test Question. Convert the Facts into a Test Question: Who? What? When? Where? Why?

_____
_____

Paragraph #
Step 1. What is the Main Idea:

_____
_____

Step 2. List Supporting Details/Examples/Arguments:

_____
_____
_____
_____
_____
_____

Step 3. Visualize the Test Question. Convert the Facts into a Test Question: Who? What? When? Why? Where?

_____
_____

SMARTGRADES: NEXT EVOLUTION BRAIN POWER REVOLUTION

Step 4. To Ace the Test, Use Association Cues to Memorize Facts for Instant and Total Recall.

Step 5: Self-Test for Strengths and Weaknesses (Change Weak Association Cues).

List Fact and Memory Association Cue

SMARTGRADES: WE ARE THE FUTURE

Date:
Chapter:
Divide and Conquer: Read One Paragraph at a Time. Number the Paragraphs.
Paragraph #
Step 1. What is the Main Idea:

_____
_____

Step 2. List Supporting Details/Examples/Arguments:

_____
_____
_____
_____
_____
_____

Step 3. Visualize the Test Question. Convert the Facts into a Test Question: Who? What? When? Where? Why?

_____
_____

Paragraph #
Step 1. What is the Main Idea:

_____
_____

Step 2. List Supporting Details/Examples/Arguments:

_____
_____
_____
_____
_____
_____

Step 3. Visualize the Test Question. Convert the Facts into a Test Question: Who? What? When? Why? Where?

_____
_____

SMARTGRADES: NEXT EVOLUTION BRAIN POWER REVOLUTION

Step 4. To Ace the Test, Use Association Cues to Memorize Facts for Instant and Total Recall.

Step 5: Self-Test for Strengths and Weaknesses (Change Weak Association Cues).

List Fact and Memory Association Cue

SMARTGRADES: WE ARE THE FUTURE

Date:
Chapter:
Divide and Conquer: Read One Paragraph at a Time. Number the Paragraphs.
Paragraph #
Step 1. What is the Main Idea:

___

Step 2. List Supporting Details/Examples/Arguments:

___

Step 3. Visualize the Test Question. Convert the Facts into a Test Question: Who? What? When? Where? Why?

___

Paragraph #
Step 1. What is the Main Idea:

___

Step 2. List Supporting Details/Examples/Arguments:

___

Step 3. Visualize the Test Question. Convert the Facts into a Test Question: Who? What? When? Why? Where?

___

SMARTGRADES: NEXT EVOLUTION BRAIN POWER REVOLUTION

Step 4. To Ace the Test, Use Association Cues to Memorize Facts for Instant and Total Recall.

Step 5: Self-Test for Strengths and Weaknesses (Change Weak Association Cues).

List Fact and Memory Association Cue

SMARTGRADES: WE ARE THE FUTURE

Date:
Chapter:
Divide and Conquer: Read One Paragraph at a Time. Number the Paragraphs.
Paragraph #
Step 1. What is the Main Idea:

_____
_____

Step 2. List Supporting Details/Examples/Arguments:

_____
_____
_____
_____
_____
_____

Step 3. Visualize the Test Question. Convert the Facts into a Test Question: Who? What? When? Where? Why?

_____
_____

Paragraph #
Step 1. What is the Main Idea:

_____
_____

Step 2. List Supporting Details/Examples/Arguments:

_____
_____
_____
_____
_____
_____

Step 3. Visualize the Test Question. Convert the Facts into a Test Question: Who? What? When? Why? Where?

_____
_____

SMARTGRADES: NEXT EVOLUTION BRAIN POWER REVOLUTION

Step 4. To Ace the Test, Use Association Cues to Memorize Facts for Instant and Total Recall.

Step 5: Self-Test for Strengths and Weaknesses (Change Weak Association Cues).

List Fact and Memory Association Cue

SMARTGRADES: WE ARE THE FUTURE

Date:
Chapter:
Divide and Conquer: Read One Paragraph at a Time. Number the Paragraphs.
Paragraph #
Step 1. What is the Main Idea:

___

Step 2. List Supporting Details/Examples/Arguments:

___

Step 3. Visualize the Test Question. Convert the Facts into a Test Question: Who? What? When? Where? Why?

___

Paragraph #
Step 1. What is the Main Idea:

___

Step 2. List Supporting Details/Examples/Arguments:

___

Step 3. Visualize the Test Question. Convert the Facts into a Test Question: Who? What? When? Why? Where?

___

SMARTGRADES: NEXT EVOLUTION BRAIN POWER REVOLUTION

Step 4. To Ace the Test, Use Association Cues to Memorize Facts for Instant and Total Recall.

Step 5: Self-Test for Strengths and Weaknesses (Change Weak Association Cues).

List Fact and Memory Association Cue

SMARTGRADES: WE ARE THE FUTURE

Date:
Chapter:
Divide and Conquer: Read One Paragraph at a Time. Number the Paragraphs.
Paragraph #
Step 1. What is the Main Idea:

_____
_____

Step 2. List Supporting Details/Examples/Arguments:

_____
_____
_____
_____
_____
_____

Step 3. Visualize the Test Question. Convert the Facts into a Test Question: Who? What? When? Where? Why?

_____
_____

Paragraph #
Step 1. What is the Main Idea:

_____
_____

Step 2. List Supporting Details/Examples/Arguments:

_____
_____
_____
_____
_____
_____

Step 3. Visualize the Test Question. Convert the Facts into a Test Question: Who? What? When? Why? Where?

_____
_____

SMARTGRADES: NEXT EVOLUTION BRAIN POWER REVOLUTION

Step 4. To Ace the Test, Use Association Cues to Memorize Facts for Instant and Total Recall.

Step 5: Self-Test for Strengths and Weaknesses (Change Weak Association Cues).

List Fact and Memory Association Cue

SMARTGRADES: WE ARE THE FUTURE

Date:
Chapter:
Divide and Conquer: Read One Paragraph at a Time. Number the Paragraphs.
Paragraph #
Step 1. What is the Main Idea:

_____
_____

Step 2. List Supporting Details/Examples/Arguments:

_____
_____
_____
_____
_____
_____

Step 3. Visualize the Test Question. Convert the Facts into a Test Question: Who? What? When? Where? Why?

_____
_____

Paragraph #
Step 1. What is the Main Idea:

_____
_____

Step 2. List Supporting Details/Examples/Arguments:

_____
_____
_____
_____
_____
_____

Step 3. Visualize the Test Question. Convert the Facts into a Test Question: Who? What? When? Why? Where?

_____
_____

SMARTGRADES: NEXT EVOLUTION BRAIN POWER REVOLUTION

Step 4. To Ace the Test, Use Association Cues to Memorize Facts for Instant and Total Recall.

Step 5: Self-Test for Strengths and Weaknesses (Change Weak Association Cues).

List Fact and Memory Association Cue

SMARTGRADES: WE ARE THE FUTURE

Date:
Chapter:
Divide and Conquer: Read One Paragraph at a Time. Number the Paragraphs.
Paragraph #
Step 1. What is the Main Idea:

_____
_____

Step 2. List Supporting Details/Examples/Arguments:

_____
_____
_____
_____
_____
_____

Step 3. Visualize the Test Question. Convert the Facts into a Test Question: Who? What? When? Where? Why?

_____
_____

Paragraph #
Step 1. What is the Main Idea:

_____
_____

Step 2. List Supporting Details/Examples/Arguments:

_____
_____
_____
_____
_____
_____

Step 3. Visualize the Test Question. Convert the Facts into a Test Question: Who? What? When? Why? Where?

_____
_____

SMARTGRADES: NEXT EVOLUTION BRAIN POWER REVOLUTION

Step 4. To Ace the Test, Use Association Cues to Memorize Facts for Instant and Total Recall.

Step 5: Self-Test for Strengths and Weaknesses (Change Weak Association Cues).

List Fact and Memory Association Cue

SMARTGRADES: WE ARE THE FUTURE

Date:
Chapter:
Divide and Conquer: Read One Paragraph at a Time. Number the Paragraphs.
Paragraph #
Step 1. What is the Main Idea:

_____
_____

Step 2. List Supporting Details/Examples/Arguments:

_____
_____
_____
_____
_____
_____

Step 3. Visualize the Test Question. Convert the Facts into a Test Question: Who? What? When? Where? Why?

_____
_____

Paragraph #
Step 1. What is the Main Idea:

_____
_____

Step 2. List Supporting Details/Examples/Arguments:

_____
_____
_____
_____
_____
_____

Step 3. Visualize the Test Question. Convert the Facts into a Test Question: Who? What? When? Why? Where?

_____
_____

SMARTGRADES: NEXT EVOLUTION BRAIN POWER REVOLUTION

Step 4. To Ace the Test, Use Association Cues to Memorize Facts for Instant and Total Recall.

Step 5: Self-Test for Strengths and Weaknesses (Change Weak Association Cues).

List Fact and Memory Association Cue

SMARTGRADES: WE ARE THE FUTURE

Date:
Chapter:
Divide and Conquer: Read One Paragraph at a Time. Number the Paragraphs.
Paragraph #
Step 1. What is the Main Idea:

_____
_____

Step 2. List Supporting Details/Examples/Arguments:

_____
_____
_____
_____
_____
_____

Step 3. Visualize the Test Question. Convert the Facts into a Test Question: Who? What? When? Where? Why?

_____
_____

Paragraph #
Step 1. What is the Main Idea:

_____
_____

Step 2. List Supporting Details/Examples/Arguments:

_____
_____
_____
_____
_____
_____

Step 3. Visualize the Test Question. Convert the Facts into a Test Question: Who? What? When? Why? Where?

_____
_____

SMARTGRADES: NEXT EVOLUTION BRAIN POWER REVOLUTION

Step 4. To Ace the Test, Use Association Cues to Memorize Facts for Instant and Total Recall.

Step 5: Self-Test for Strengths and Weaknesses (Change Weak Association Cues).

List Fact and Memory Association Cue

SMARTGRADES: WE ARE THE FUTURE

Date:
Chapter:
Divide and Conquer: Read One Paragraph at a Time. Number the Paragraphs.
Paragraph #
Step 1. What is the Main Idea:

_____
_____

Step 2. List Supporting Details/Examples/Arguments:

_____
_____
_____
_____
_____
_____

Step 3. Visualize the Test Question. Convert the Facts into a Test Question: Who? What? When? Where? Why?

_____
_____

Paragraph #
Step 1. What is the Main Idea:

_____
_____

Step 2. List Supporting Details/Examples/Arguments:

_____
_____
_____
_____
_____
_____

Step 3. Visualize the Test Question. Convert the Facts into a Test Question: Who? What? When? Why? Where?

_____
_____

SMARTGRADES: NEXT EVOLUTION BRAIN POWER REVOLUTION

Step 4. To Ace the Test, Use Association Cues to Memorize Facts for Instant and Total Recall.

Step 5: Self-Test for Strengths and Weaknesses (Change Weak Association Cues).

List Fact and Memory Association Cue

SMARTGRADES: WE ARE THE FUTURE

Date:
Chapter:
Divide and Conquer: Read One Paragraph at a Time. Number the Paragraphs.
Paragraph #
Step 1. What is the Main Idea:

_____
_____

Step 2. List Supporting Details/Examples/Arguments:

_____
_____
_____
_____
_____
_____

Step 3. Visualize the Test Question. Convert the Facts into a Test Question: Who? What? When? Where? Why?

_____
_____

Paragraph #
Step 1. What is the Main Idea:

_____
_____

Step 2. List Supporting Details/Examples/Arguments:

_____
_____
_____
_____
_____
_____

Step 3. Visualize the Test Question. Convert the Facts into a Test Question: Who? What? When? Why? Where?

_____
_____

SMARTGRADES: NEXT EVOLUTION BRAIN POWER REVOLUTION

Step 4. To Ace the Test, Use Association Cues to Memorize Facts for Instant and Total Recall.

Step 5: Self-Test for Strengths and Weaknesses (Change Weak Association Cues).

List Fact and Memory Association Cue

SMARTGRADES: WE ARE THE FUTURE

Date:
Chapter:
Divide and Conquer: Read One Paragraph at a Time. Number the Paragraphs.
Paragraph #
Step 1. What is the Main Idea:

_____
_____

Step 2. List Supporting Details/Examples/Arguments:

_____
_____
_____
_____
_____
_____

Step 3. Visualize the Test Question. Convert the Facts into a Test Question: Who? What? When? Where? Why?

_____
_____

Paragraph #
Step 1. What is the Main Idea:

_____
_____

Step 2. List Supporting Details/Examples/Arguments:

_____
_____
_____
_____
_____
_____

Step 3. Visualize the Test Question. Convert the Facts into a Test Question: Who? What? When? Why? Where?

_____
_____

SMARTGRADES: NEXT EVOLUTION BRAIN POWER REVOLUTION

Step 4. To Ace the Test, Use Association Cues to Memorize Facts for Instant and Total Recall.

Step 5: Self-Test for Strengths and Weaknesses (Change Weak Association Cues).

List Fact and Memory Association Cue

SMARTGRADES: WE ARE THE FUTURE

Date:
Chapter:
Divide and Conquer: Read One Paragraph at a Time. Number the Paragraphs.
Paragraph #
Step 1. What is the Main Idea:

_____
_____

Step 2. List Supporting Details/Examples/Arguments:

_____
_____
_____
_____
_____

Step 3. Visualize the Test Question. Convert the Facts into a Test Question: Who? What? When? Where? Why?

_____
_____

Paragraph #
Step 1. What is the Main Idea:

_____
_____

Step 2. List Supporting Details/Examples/Arguments:

_____
_____
_____
_____
_____

Step 3. Visualize the Test Question. Convert the Facts into a Test Question: Who? What? When? Why? Where?

_____
_____

SMARTGRADES: NEXT EVOLUTION BRAIN POWER REVOLUTION

Step 4. To Ace the Test, Use Association Cues to Memorize Facts for Instant and Total Recall.

Step 5: Self-Test for Strengths and Weaknesses (Change Weak Association Cues).

List Fact and Memory Association Cue

SMARTGRADES: WE ARE THE FUTURE

Date:
Chapter:
Divide and Conquer: Read One Paragraph at a Time. Number the Paragraphs.
Paragraph #
Step 1. What is the Main Idea:

_____
_____

Step 2. List Supporting Details/Examples/Arguments:

_____
_____
_____
_____
_____
_____

Step 3. Visualize the Test Question. Convert the Facts into a Test Question: Who? What? When? Where? Why?

_____
_____

Paragraph #
Step 1. What is the Main Idea:

_____
_____

Step 2. List Supporting Details/Examples/Arguments:

_____
_____
_____
_____
_____
_____

Step 3. Visualize the Test Question. Convert the Facts into a Test Question: Who? What? When? Why? Where?

_____
_____

SMARTGRADES: NEXT EVOLUTION BRAIN POWER REVOLUTION

Step 4. To Ace the Test, Use Association Cues to Memorize Facts for Instant and Total Recall.

Step 5: Self-Test for Strengths and Weaknesses (Change Weak Association Cues).

List Fact and Memory Association Cue

SMARTGRADES: WE ARE THE FUTURE

Date:
Chapter:
Divide and Conquer: Read One Paragraph at a Time. Number the Paragraphs.
Paragraph #
Step 1. What is the Main Idea:

_____
_____

Step 2. List Supporting Details/Examples/Arguments:

_____
_____
_____
_____
_____
_____

Step 3. Visualize the Test Question. Convert the Facts into a Test Question: Who? What? When? Where? Why?

_____
_____

Paragraph #
Step 1. What is the Main Idea:

_____
_____

Step 2. List Supporting Details/Examples/Arguments:

_____
_____
_____
_____
_____
_____

Step 3. Visualize the Test Question. Convert the Facts into a Test Question: Who? What? When? Why? Where?

_____
_____

SMARTGRADES: NEXT EVOLUTION BRAIN POWER REVOLUTION

Step 4. To Ace the Test, Use Association Cues to Memorize Facts for Instant and Total Recall.

Step 5: Self-Test for Strengths and Weaknesses (Change Weak Association Cues).

List Fact and Memory Association Cue

SMARTGRADES: WE ARE THE FUTURE

Date:
Chapter:
Divide and Conquer: Read One Paragraph at a Time. Number the Paragraphs.
Paragraph #
Step 1. What is the Main Idea:
_____
_____

Step 2. List Supporting Details/Examples/Arguments:
_____
_____
_____
_____
_____
_____

Step 3. Visualize the Test Question. Convert the Facts into a Test Question: Who? What? When? Where? Why?
_____
_____

Paragraph #
Step 1. What is the Main Idea:
_____
_____

Step 2. List Supporting Details/Examples/Arguments:
_____
_____
_____
_____
_____
_____

Step 3. Visualize the Test Question. Convert the Facts into a Test Question: Who? What? When? Why? Where?
_____
_____

SMARTGRADES: NEXT EVOLUTION BRAIN POWER REVOLUTION

Step 4. To Ace the Test, Use Association Cues to Memorize Facts for Instant and Total Recall.

Step 5: Self-Test for Strengths and Weaknesses (Change Weak Association Cues).

List Fact and Memory Association Cue

SMARTGRADES: WE ARE THE FUTURE

Date:
Chapter:
Divide and Conquer: Read One Paragraph at a Time. Number the Paragraphs.
Paragraph #
Step 1. What is the Main Idea:

_____
_____

Step 2. List Supporting Details/Examples/Arguments:

_____
_____
_____
_____
_____
_____

Step 3. Visualize the Test Question. Convert the Facts into a Test Question: Who? What? When? Where? Why?

_____
_____

Paragraph #
Step 1. What is the Main Idea:

_____
_____

Step 2. List Supporting Details/Examples/Arguments:

_____
_____
_____
_____
_____
_____

Step 3. Visualize the Test Question. Convert the Facts into a Test Question: Who? What? When? Why? Where?

_____
_____

SMARTGRADES: NEXT EVOLUTION BRAIN POWER REVOLUTION

Step 4. To Ace the Test, Use Association Cues to Memorize Facts for Instant and Total Recall.

Step 5: Self-Test for Strengths and Weaknesses (Change Weak Association Cues).

List Fact and Memory Association Cue

SMARTGRADES: WE ARE THE FUTURE

Date:
Chapter:
Divide and Conquer: Read One Paragraph at a Time. Number the Paragraphs.
Paragraph #
Step 1. What is the Main Idea:
_____
_____

Step 2. List Supporting Details/Examples/Arguments:
_____
_____
_____
_____
_____
_____

Step 3. Visualize the Test Question. Convert the Facts into a Test Question: Who? What? When? Where? Why?
_____
_____

Paragraph #
Step 1. What is the Main Idea:
_____
_____

Step 2. List Supporting Details/Examples/Arguments:
_____
_____
_____
_____
_____
_____

Step 3. Visualize the Test Question. Convert the Facts into a Test Question: Who? What? When? Why? Where?
_____
_____

SMARTGRADES: NEXT EVOLUTION BRAIN POWER REVOLUTION

Step 4. To Ace the Test, Use Association Cues to Memorize Facts for Instant and Total Recall.

Step 5: Self-Test for Strengths and Weaknesses (Change Weak Association Cues).

List Fact and Memory Association Cue

SMARTGRADES: WE ARE THE FUTURE

Date:
Chapter:
Divide and Conquer: Read One Paragraph at a Time. Number the Paragraphs.
Paragraph #
Step 1. What is the Main Idea:
_____
_____

Step 2. List Supporting Details/Examples/Arguments:
_____
_____
_____
_____
_____
_____

Step 3. Visualize the Test Question. Convert the Facts into a Test Question: Who? What? When? Where? Why?
_____
_____

Paragraph #
Step 1. What is the Main Idea:
_____
_____

Step 2. List Supporting Details/Examples/Arguments:
_____
_____
_____
_____
_____
_____

Step 3. Visualize the Test Question. Convert the Facts into a Test Question: Who? What? When? Why? Where?
_____
_____

SMARTGRADES: NEXT EVOLUTION BRAIN POWER REVOLUTION

Step 4. To Ace the Test, Use Association Cues to Memorize Facts for Instant and Total Recall.

Step 5: Self-Test for Strengths and Weaknesses (Change Weak Association Cues).

List Fact and Memory Association Cue

Our Power Study Snack Suggestions

Choose One of Our Power Study Snacks or Create Your Own Energy Menu

1. **Nutritious Pizza** ✓
   Whole Wheat Pita, Mozzarella Cheese Slice, Tomato Slice, Basil Leaf, and Olive Oil
   Microwave 30 Seconds

2. **Humus and Veggies** ✓
   Carrots, Celery, Broccoli, Red Peppers . . .

3. **Bran Muffin** ✓
   Apple-Oat, Cranberry-Walnut, Banana-Pecan . . .

4. **Sports Bar with 10+ Grams of Protein** ✓
   Avoid High Amounts of Saturated Fat or Hydrogenated Vegetable Oils

5. **A Small 3oz. Can of Tuna/Sardines with 4-6 Whole Grain Crackers** ✓

6. **One Container of Low Fat Yogurt Sprinkled with High Fiber Cereal and Fresh Fruit** ✓

7. **Whole-Grain Cereal with Fat Free or 1% Low Fat Milk and Fresh Fruit** ✓

8. **Trail Mix: Your Favorite Nuts** ✓
   Peanuts, Almonds, Cashews, Pistachios with Raisins and Cranberries . . .

9. **Dried Fruit Mix: Your Favorite Fruits** ✓
   Apricots, Pineapple, Apple Chips, Banana Chips . . .

10. **Vegetable Soup and a Slice of Whole Grain Bread** ✓

11. **Chocolate Smoothie: Chocolate Soy Milk, Peanut Butter, and Whey Protein** ✓

12. **Oatmeal-Raisin Cookie** ✓

SMARTGRADES:NEXT EVOLUTION BRAIN POWER REVOLUTION

My Power Study Snacks

List Your Favorite Power Study Snacks to Stay Energized and Focused

1. _____

2. _____

3. _____

4. _____

5. _____

6. _____

7. _____

8. _____

9. _____

10. _____

PHOTON
SUPERHERO of EDUCATION®

EVERY DAY AN EASY A

EVERY DAY AN EASY A
3 Editions: Elementary, High School, College
ACE EVERY TEST EVERY TIME
All Global Bookstores

www.BooksNotBombs.com
EVERYBODY IS SOMEBODY SPECIAL

1 Minute Time Management Class
10 Steps to Success
EVERY DAY AN EASY A ©All Rights Reserved, 2010.

Step 1 ☐
Make a Daily Action Plan
Write Down Your Big Goals

Step 2 ☐
Set Your Priorities
Urgent, Important, Low, and Optional

Step 3 ☐
Breakdown Your Dreams
Breakdown Big Goal into Smaller Steps
List Steps Necessary to Complete Big Goal

Step 4 ☐
Divide and Conquer
Take Baby Steps Toward Reaching Goal
Crawl. Walk. Fly. Soar...

Step 5 ☐
Use Time Logs: Estimated Vs. Actual Time
e.g., Estimate Time for Lunch: 1 Hour
Actual Time: 20 Minutes
40 Minutes for Errands: Bank, Post Office, Store

Step 6 ☐
Life Is a Bumpy Road
Make Time for Delays, Detours,
Distractions, and Disappointments
e.g., Copier Runs Out of Toner and Paper

Step 7 ☐
Use Checkboxes to Keep Track of Completed Tasks

Step 8 ☐
Review and Refine Daily Action Plan
Pay Attention to Strengths and Weaknesses

Step 9 ☐
Celebrate Your Success
Celebrate Job Well Done with Daily Reward

Step 10 ☐
EVERY DAY AN EASY A
www.everydayaneasya.com